HAL•LEONARD
INSTRUMENTAL
PLAY-ALONG

AUDIO
ACCESS
INCLUDED

MANNHEIM STEAMROLLER
Christmas

To access audio visit:
www.halleonard.com/mylibrary

Enter Code
1451-2645-8667-1784

Audio Arrangements by Peter Deneff

ISBN 978-1-4803-9707-1

HAL•LEONARD®
CORPORATION

7777 W. BLUEMOUND RD. P.O. BOX 13819 MILWAUKEE, WI 53213

In Australia Contact:
Hal Leonard Australia Pty. Ltd.
4 Lentara Court
Cheltenham, Victoria, 3192 Australia
Email: ausadmin@halleonard.com.au

Visit Hal Leonard Online at
www.halleonard.com

CONTENTS

BRING A TORCH, JEANETTE ISABELLA

ALTO SAX

17th Century French Provencal Carol
Arranged by CHIP DAVIS

GOOD KING WENCESLAS

ALTO SAX

Arranged by CHIP DAVIS

CAROL OF THE BELLS

Ukrainian Christmas Carol
Arranged by CHIP DAVIS

ALTO SAX

CHRISTMAS LULLABY

ALTO SAX

By CHIP DAVIS

DECK THE HALLS

ALTO SAX

Arranged by CHIP DAVIS

GOD REST YE MERRY GENTLEMEN

ALTO SAX

19th Century English Carol
Arranged by CHIP DAVIS

GREENSLEEVES

ALTO SAX

Sixteenth Century Traditional English
Arranged by CHIP DAVIS

HARK! THE HERALD ANGELS SING

ALTO SAX

By FELIX MENDELSSOHN
Arranged by CHIP DAVIS

JOY TO THE WORLD

ALTO SAX

Arranged by CHIP DAVIS

PAT A PAN

ALTO SAX

Words and Music by BERNARD DE LA MONNOYE
Arranged by CHIP DAVIS

SILENT NIGHT

ALTO SAX

Arranged by CHIP DAVIS

TRADITIONS OF CHRISTMAS

ALTO SAX

By CHIP DAVIS